A TRUE BOOK™

THE EARTH AT RISK

GRASSLANDS IN DANGER

Felicia Brower

Children's Press®
An imprint of Scholastic Inc.

Content Consultant
Carl Wepking, Ph.D.
University of Wisconsin–Madison
Department of Plant and Agroecosystem Sciences
with thanks to Marion Wepking for providing a kid's perspective as well

Library of Congress Cataloging-in-Publication Data available

ISBN 978-93-5954-252-2

Printed in India at Polykam Offset New Delhi 110028

This reprint edition, October 2024

Design by Kathleen Petelinsek
Series produced by Spooky Cheetah Press

Front cover: Grasslands face many threats, including drought, more intense wildfires, and development.

Find the Truth!

Everything you are about to read is true ***except*** for one of the sentences on this page.

Which one is **TRUE**?

T or F Grasslands cover about 25 percent of Earth.

T or F Grassland soils are nutrient-poor.

Find the answers in this book.

What's in This Book?

In spring and summer, temperate grasslands are covered in wildflowers.

People are working to protect our grasslands.

The BIG Truth

The Carbon Keepers

3 Grasslands Under Threat

Giraffes live in temperate and tropical grasslands.

INTRODUCTION

Grasslands are windy, open, mostly flat areas of land covered mainly by—you guessed it—**grass**! Rain doesn't fall consistently enough in this **biome** to support many tall plants or trees. But grasslands get enough rain for **grass**, **flowers**, and **small shrubs** to **flourish**.

The combination of dry grass and high winds means **wildfires are fairly common** here. Yet many plants and animals make their homes in grasslands around the world. These areas even help fight **climate change**. However, grasslands—and the animals that live there—are currently at risk due to human activity. Luckily people are working to help save these wild places.

Cheetahs live in the tropical grasslands of Africa.

Wildfires are part of a healthy grassland life cycle. However, uncontrolled wildfires pose a serious threat.

Grasslands Around the World

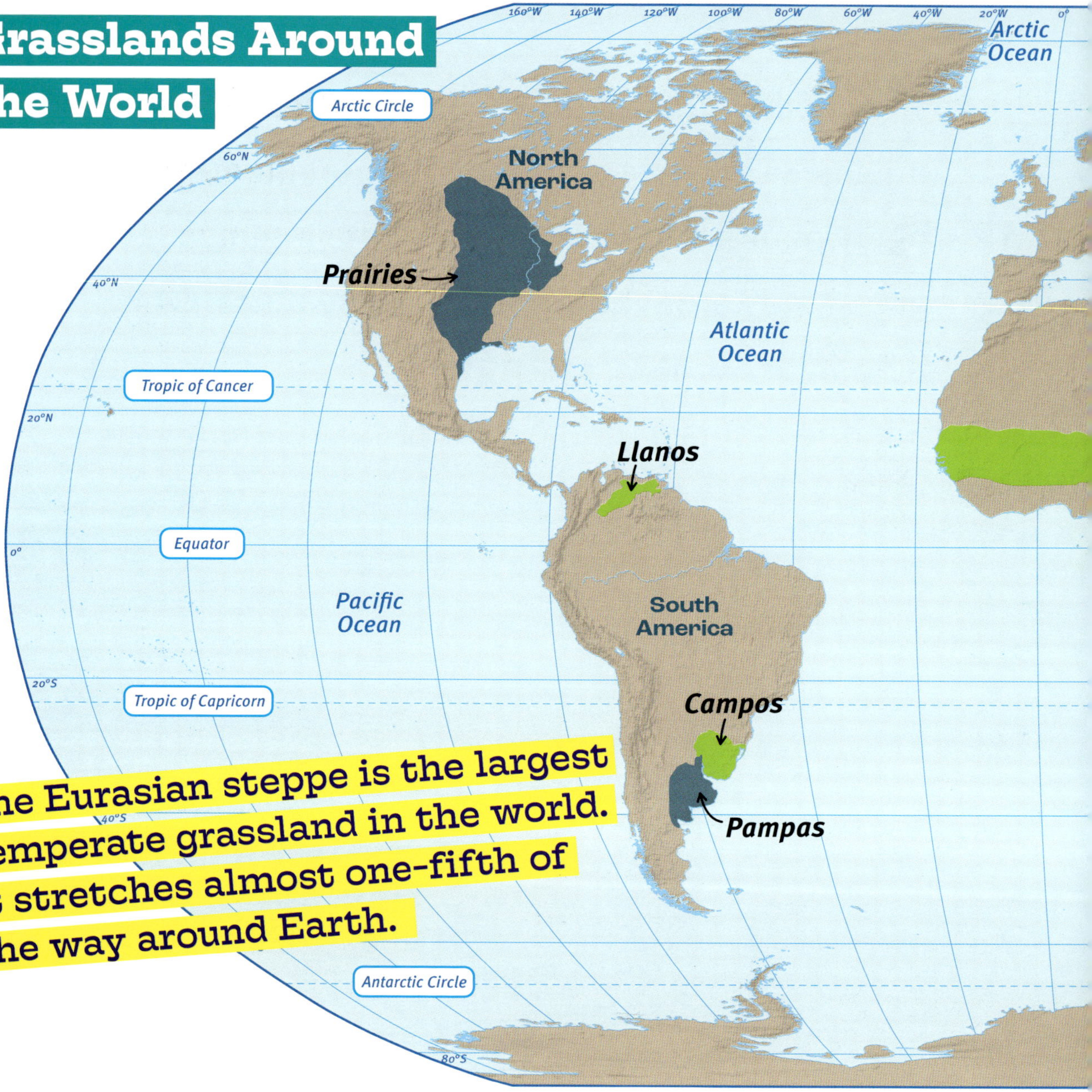

The Eurasian steppe is the largest temperate grassland in the world. It stretches almost one-fifth of the way around Earth.

There are two main **types of grasslands**: **tropical** and **temperate**. The main differences between the two are **temperature** and **annual rainfall**.

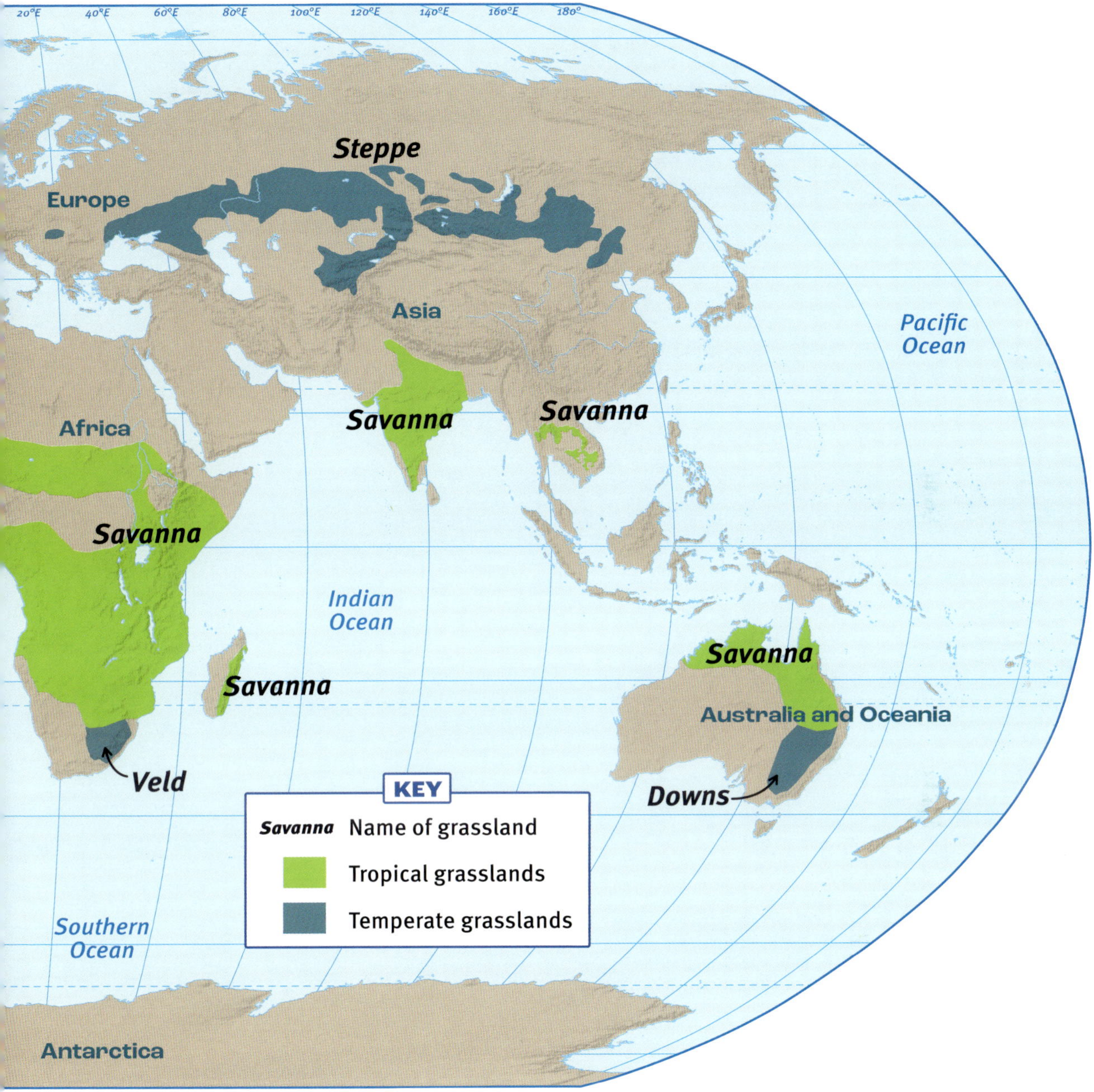

Grasslands are found on **every continent except Antarctica**. They have different names in different places, as well as animals that are unique to each.

These photos show tropical grasslands in Australia during the wet season (top) and dry season (bottom).

The first grasses and grasslands formed in Africa and South America.

CHAPTER

1

Tropical Grasslands

Tropical grasslands are warm all year long. They have two seasons: wet and dry. Up to 50 inches (127 centimeters) of rain can fall during the wet season. During the dry season, there may be no rain at all for months at a time. A wide variety of grasses and other plants thrive in tropical grasslands. That enables this **ecosystem** to support a large and varied wildlife population.

The Grass Isn't Always Greener

Red oat, bluestem, and elephant are all types of grasses that can be found in tropical grasslands around the world. During the dry season, grasses will often go **dormant** to survive the heat and lack of water. The grass might look dead, but the roots are still alive underground. The grasses will turn green again when it rains.

An acacia tree can store up to 32 gallons (121 liters) of water in its roots.

Tough Trees

Trees in tropical grasslands have also adapted to survive the dry season. In Africa, acacia trees have long roots that can reach water deep underground. Baobab trees have large, thick trunks that store water. The eucalyptus is native to Australia. During the dry season it may shed some leaves and twigs to conserve water.

In the African Savanna

Africa's tropical grasslands can support many herbivores, like gazelles, zebras, and wildebeests. Often, the animals eat different plants or different parts of plants. For example, giraffes often eat the highest leaves on trees and shrubs. Impalas browse on leaves that are lower down. Meat-eaters such as lions, cheetahs, leopards, and hyenas are found nearby. They eat herbivores.

The Great Grassland Migration

Every year, about two million animals, including zebras, wildebeests, and gazelles, travel more than 1,000 miles (1,609 kilometers) in a loop through East Africa. They are following the rains in search of fresh grass to eat and good supplies of water. The journey starts at the end of Tanzania's wet season. The animals set out from Tanzania's savanna, which is called the Serengeti. They are heading north for the Masai Mara, the savanna in Kenya, where the rains come a little later. As the wet season ends in Kenya, the animals will head back south to Tanzania. The trip is not easy. The **migrating** mammals have to cross the Mara River—and survive the crocodiles—to make it to their feeding grounds.

zebras and wildebeests

About 250,000 animals die each year from exhaustion, drowning, or being eaten by **predators**.

Wildebeests cross the Mara River during the Great Migration—the largest migration of mammals on Earth.

In the Australian Savanna

A variety of **marsupials** are found in Australia's tropical grasslands. They include kangaroos, wombats, and koalas. Kangaroos and wombats eat grass and shrubs. Koalas eat leaves—mainly eucalyptus. The dingo is one of Australia's top predators. This wild dog hunts small mammals. It also works in packs to take down large animals like kangaroos.

kangaroos

wombat

koala

dingo

Kangaroo babies grow outside their mother's bodies—in a pouch.

In Campos and Llanos

In South America, more than 100 mammal species live in tropical grasslands, including capybaras and jaguars. That is also where the arrau turtle can be found. It is the largest freshwater turtle in South America. The black spot piranha lives in the Orinoco River, which runs through the grasslands. The piranha uses its razor-sharp teeth to feed on other fish and birds.

North America's prairies change with the seasons.

Temperate means the weather is in the middle—not too hot and not too cold.

CHAPTER 2

Temperate Grasslands

Temperate grasslands have four seasons. Summers are hot, and winters can be cold and snowy. The grasslands may receive up to 35 in. (89 cm) of rain and snow a year. When the weather is warm, the land is covered in colorful vegetation. Each winter when the plants go dormant, they break down and add nutrients to the soil. The animals that live there change with the seasons too. Some grow thicker coats to stay warm. Others dig burrows to keep out of the snow.

Survival of the Fittest

Purple needlegrass, wild oats, foxtail, buffalo grass, and ryegrass all grow in temperate grasslands around the world. These grasses send up new blades from a place on the plant that is very close to the ground. They can continue to grow even after many animals have grazed on them.

The ombu is the only treelike plant that grows in South American grasslands. It has a fire-resistant trunk that stores water.

Because wildfires are common in grasslands, plants found there often have stems and buds that grow underground. Even fire cannot destroy them. Grasslands also experience strong winds. Many plants that grow there are close to the ground so they won't get ripped up by the wind.

Today, most of the prairies that used to cover North America are gone.

In the Prairies

Bison are the largest mammals found in North America's temperate grasslands. They use their huge heads and necks as snowplows to uncover grass in winter. Prairie dogs are some of the smaller grasslands mammals. They dig vast networks of underground burrows for protection from predators such as hawks.

In the Pampas

The greater rhea is a flightless bird that lives in the temperate grasslands of South America. It stands 5 feet (1.5 meters) tall. The bird's long legs help it see over tall grasses to spot predators. Of course, some predators, like the maned wolf, have long legs too! Some animals, like the guanaco and Geoffroy's cat, have coats that help them blend into the pampas grasses.

In the Velds

Many herbivores live in Africa's temperate grasslands, including elephants and black rhinos. Elephants and rhinoceroses eat leaves and tree bark. Elephants also eat grass. Lions, cheetahs, leopards, and hyenas stalk the grasslands hunting prey. The black mamba snake also lives in the velds. It is one of the deadliest animals in the world.

Many animals that live in Africa's tropical savannas also live in the temperate velds.

In the Downs

The critically **endangered** plains-wanderer is found in Australia's temperate grasslands. This small bird's brown, spotted feathers help it blend in with its grassy surroundings. The downs are also the only place where the Victorian grassland earless dragon is found. Before 2023, this lizard hadn't been seen there in 50 years.

In the Steppes

The grasslands that stretch from Hungary in Europe to China in Asia are known as the Steppes. The eastern steppes support more than one million Mongolian gazelles. That is where you'll also find unique animals like the pallas cat and saiga antelope. The saiga's large nose helps it survive in the steppes. It filters dust out of the air in summer and warms up cold air in winter.

A large number of rodents live in the steppes. They include hamsters and marmots. Both animals dig burrows underground to hide from predators like the steppe eagle. By creating burrows, the animals are also helping the ecosystem. Their digging stirs up and adds nutrients to the soil.

The word *steppe* comes from a Russian word that means "flat grassy plain."

The BIG Truth

The Carbon Keepers

Our climate is changing because of global warming. Human activities are creating excess carbon dioxide (CO_2) that is released into our atmosphere, which is causing our planet to heat up. Carbon sequestration is one way to slow global warming— and climate change. This is why grasslands are so effective at carbon sequestration:

1

CO_2 is released into the atmosphere mainly when we burn fossil fuels, like coal and oil. These fuels are burned to create electricity for our houses and buildings, and power for our cars.

2

Like all plants, grasses take in CO_2 from the atmosphere during **photosynthesis**. They release oxygen (O_2) back into the air. But when it comes to grassland plants, much of the carbon gets stored deep underground in the grasses' long roots and in the soil. This is different from how other plants store carbon. For example, trees store carbon in their trunks, branches, leaves, and roots.

3

The carbon is stored—or *sequestered*—until the plant dies. When grass dies, the carbon is released into the soil as the roots break down. It is not released back into the atmosphere—even if the grass is destroyed by fire. By sequestering a lot of carbon in the soil, grasslands strongly contribute to slowing global warming. On the other hand, when a tree dies or burns in a fire, some of the carbon stored in its trunk, branches, or leaves is re-released into the atmosphere instead of being stored in the soil. Trees are not as effective at sequestering carbon.

photosynthesis

carbon sequestered

Humans work in the opposite way of plants. When we breathe, we take in oxygen and release carbon dioxide.

Up to 80 percent of all wildfires on Earth occur in grasslands.

Drought can destroy grasslands (top). It can also increase the risk of intense wildfires (bottom).

CHAPTER

3

Grasslands Under Threat

Grasslands face many different threats, most of which are caused by humans. Because grasslands tend to be flat, wide-open spaces, people around the world have converted them into farmland, towns, and cities. Destructive droughts and wildfires, which are worsened by the impacts of climate change, also wipe out grasslands and the animals that live there. Some of these animals are endangered. Thankfully, there are things we can do to take action before it is too late.

The Alarming Side of Farming

The soil found in grasslands is full of nutrients. That makes it ideal for growing crops and for providing grazing land for livestock. In fact, 20 percent of the world's native grasslands are now used for agriculture. Millions of acres of African savanna are lost each year due to farming and **overgrazing**.

Cows grazing on the South American pampas

Meet the Maasai People of East Africa

The Maasai People have lived in the tropical grasslands of Kenya and Tanzania—and have herded their cattle and goats there—for hundreds of years. They have been able to maintain their traditional lifestyle without destroying the land. One way they do this is by moving their herds seasonally. That keeps the grasslands from becoming overgrazed. Drought and loss of grasslands from development have made it hard for the Maasai to herd their livestock. To help keep their food supply high, they're learning how to farm crops that do well in an environment without a lot of water.

About one million Maasai people live in East Africa.

Growing Out of Control

Invasive species are also threatening grasslands. An invasive species is a plant or an animal that is introduced to an area where it had not previously been found. It often uses up the available resources, like food and water. That can cause native plants and animals to die. An invasive animal might also prey on native species.

Invasive species are often introduced by people—either accidentally or on purpose.

Aggressive woody plants such as rubber vine and tree of heaven are a problem for grasslands. They break up large stretches of grass, reducing habitats for plants and animals. Some other invasive plants, like common barberry, carry disease. European rabbits have caused big problems in Australia. The rabbits hurt native animals and plants. And they have no natural predators in Australia, so they continue to multiply.

Illegal Hunting

Illegal hunters are also called poachers. Sometimes poachers will hunt grassland animals for food. Sometimes they hunt them to sell certain body parts. For example, elephants are killed for the ivory in their tusks. Cheetahs are killed for their fur. Illegal hunting puts entire species at risk.

Timeline: Grasslands Through History

66 MILLION YEARS AGO
The first grasses appear during the Cretaceous period.

3 MILLION YEARS AGO
Grasslands spread through the Isthmus of Panama, allowing plants and animals to migrate between North and South America.

12,000 YEARS AGO
Humans begin to clear and cultivate grasslands for farming.

11,550 YEARS AGO
The Pleistocene Ice Age ends, leading to warming temperatures worldwide and shrinking grasslands.

Dangerous Fires

Fires are part of a grassland's natural life cycle. They help this biome by burning fallen leaves and returning important nutrients to the soil. But when blazes get out of control, they can cause a lot of damage. Drought conditions caused by climate change have made uncontrolled wildfires more common in the world's grasslands.

1800s
The Agricultural Revolution leads to even more grasslands being changed into farms.

EARLY 1900s
The invention of the combine harvester makes it easier to harvest crops and speeds up how fast grasslands are turned into farmland.

2000s
More grasslands are turned into farms or housing for a growing worldwide human population.

TODAY
About 25 percent of the world is covered in grasslands, but only about 5 percent is protected. The remaining 20 percent is at risk.

Getting Grasslands Back

All around the world, government agencies, conservation groups, and people like you are working to slow down or reverse grassland destruction. In some areas, farmers are paid *not* to plant crops. Instead, they plant native grasses and wildflowers. Other landowners make sure that no one can ever build on their land or make a farm there. Because the land is undeveloped, it can become grasslands again naturally.

This farmer has planted wildflowers on part of his land.

These women are working on prairie restoration in Iowa.

What You Can Do

You've taken the first step toward protecting our planet's grasslands just by reading this book. Now share what you've learned with others. The more people know about this biome, the more likely they will be to protect it. We can make a change if we all work together!

Amazing Comeback

Up to one million black-footed ferrets used to roam across North America's prairies from Canada to Northern Mexico. But by the late 1950s, due to grassland destruction, experts believed the species was **extinct**. Then, in 1981, researchers discovered a small population of ferrets living in Wyoming. They captured 18 individuals to start a breeding colony. Today, there are 600 black-footed ferrets living in North America that are all descended from those 18 animals. Still, the black-footed ferret is one of North America's most endangered mammals.

Black-footed ferrets are the only ferrets native to North America.

Kid Heroes

Avryl Fred, from Modena, New York, is passionate about helping the environment. In 2023, Avryl volunteered at the Shawangunk Grasslands National Wildlife Refuge (SGNWR) in Wallkill, New York. The refuge was established to support migrating birds that depend on grasslands for their survival.

1

Q: What inspired you to volunteer at SGNWR?

A: I've always been interested in nature and wanted to help the environment. My dream is to become some kind of ecologist when I grow up. Grassland ecosystems are important to save. They are biodiverse and beautiful—full of different kinds of bugs, birds, and plants, including some that live only in this biome.

2

Q: What did a typical day as a volunteer look like for you?

A: I worked with a biology intern named Hannah on a project to identify invasive species, such as autumn olive, multiflora rose, and glossy buckthorn. Hannah had an iPad with a satellite image of the grassland that was split up into a grid. In every square of the grid we had to identify the invasive species (if there were any) and note how many of each there were.

3

Q: Any words of advice for other kids who want to start volunteering?

A: You're never too young to make a difference. A great way to get involved is by participating in citizen science projects like the Great Backyard Bird Count or recording your observations in an app like iNaturalist. You can also check to see if your local parks or preserves have any opportunities or programs that you can help with. You can also do what I do and carry a notebook around to record your observations—that's science! Every little thing helps.

True Statistics*

Percentage of Earth that is covered by grasslands: About 25%

Percentage of protected grasslands around the world: About 5%

Number of continents with grasslands: 6

Number of acres of grasslands on Earth: 11 billion

Size of the largest temperate grassland: 3.9 million square miles (10 million sq. km)—the Eurasian steppe

Annual rainfall in tropical grasslands: Up to 50 inches (127 cm)

Annual rainfall and snow in temperate grasslands: 20 to 35 inches (51 to 89 cm)

Location of most tropical grasslands: 10 to 20 degrees latitude north and south of the equator

Height range of grassland grasses: From 1 foot (30.5 cm) to 7 feet (2.1 m)

*As of 2024

Did you find the truth?

T Grasslands cover about 25 percent of Earth.

F Grassland soils are nutrient-poor.

Resources

Other books in this series:

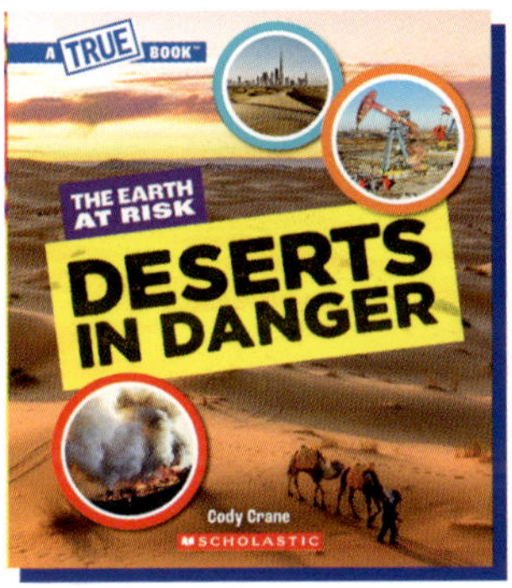

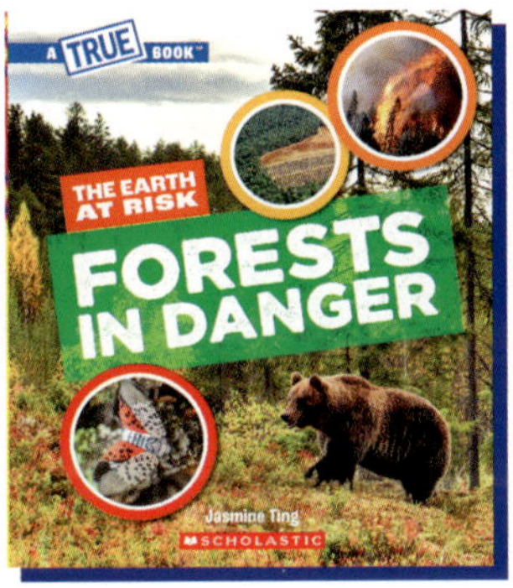

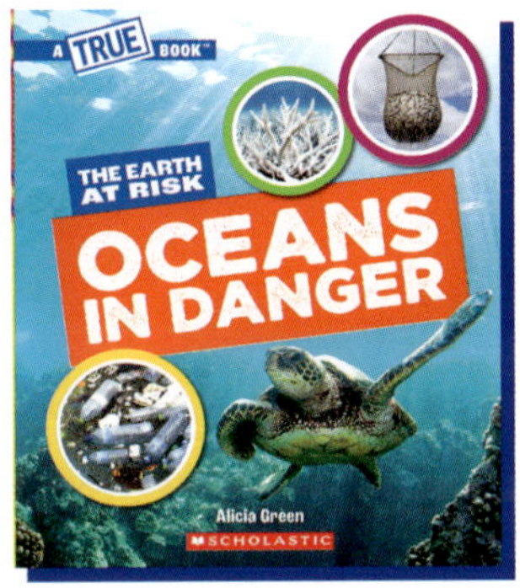

You can also look at:

Free, Katie. *Understanding Climate Change: Animals in Danger*. New York: Scholastic, 2020.

Gardeski, Christina Mia. *All About Grasslands*. United Kingdom: Raintree, 2019.

Johansson, Philip. *The Grasslands: Discover This Wide Open Biome*. New York: Enslow, 2014.

Stille, Darlene R. *Grasslands*. New York: Scholastic, 2000.

Glossary

biome (BYE-ohm) a region of the world with similar animals and plants

climate change (KLYE-mit CHAYNJ) global warming and other changes in the weather and weather patterns that are happening because of human activity

dormant (DOR-muhnt) a plant or seed that is alive but not growing

ecosystem (EE-koh-sis-tuhm) all the living things in a place and their relation to their environment

endangered (en-DAYN-jurd) in danger of becoming extinct, usually because of human activity

extinct (ik-STINGKT) no longer found alive

marsupials (mahr-SOO-pee-uhlz) any of a large group of animals in which females carry their babies in pouches on their abdomens

migrating (MYE-gray-ting) moving to another area or climate at a particular time of year

overgrazing (oh-vur-GRAY-zing) allowing animals to graze an area to the point of damaging or destroying the vegetation

photosynthesis (foh-toh-SIN-thi-sis) a chemical process by which plants and some other organisms make their food

predators (PRED-uh-turz) animals that live by hunting other animals for food

Index

Page numbers in **bold** indicate illustrations.

About the Author

Felicia Brower is a writer living in Denver, Colorado, who is passionate about conservation and the environment. She studied Environmental Policy and Planning at Virginia Tech and loves learning about and sharing ways to protect ecosystems around the world.

Photos ©: cover background: David Lazar/Getty Images; cover top right: John Dambik/Alamy Images; back cover: Hernan Caputo/Getty Images; 3: Ayzenstayn/Getty Images; 4: KenCanning/Getty Images; 5 top: Sundry Photography/Getty Images; 5 bottom: Art Wolfe/Getty Images; 6–7: WLDavies/Getty Images; 8–9: Jim McMahon/Mapman ®; 10–11 top: Auscape/Universal Images Group/Getty Images; 10–11 bottom: Auscape/Universal Images Group/Getty Images; 12 left: Mamik Slamet Asrori/Getty Images; 12 right: luxiangjian4711/Getty Images; 13 main: Ayzenstayn/Getty Images; 13 inset top: Tuul & Bruno Morandi/Getty Images; 13 inset bottom: Yvonne Van der Horst/Getty Images; 14 center top: Art Wolfe/Getty Images; 14 center bottom: Gerald Corsi/Getty Images; 15 main: O. Alamany & E. Vicens/Getty Images; 15 inset: Suzi Eszterhas/Minden Pictures; 16 center top: Posnov/Getty Images; 17 top inset: marktucan/Getty Images; 18 top left: john finney photography/Getty Images; 18 bottom left: KenCanning/Getty Images; 18–19 top: KenCanning/Getty Images; 20 top left: Amphawan Chanunpha/Getty Images; 20 bottom: ma-no/Getty Images; 21 left: Frank Hecker/Alamy Images; 21 right: Teresa Grau Ros; 22 main: Gerald Corsi/Getty Images; 22 top inset: W. Perry Conway/Getty Images; 23 top: Its About Light/Design Pics/Getty Images; 23 center top: Mark Jones/age fotostock; 23 center bottom: Hernan Caputo/Getty Images; 23 bottom: Juniors Bildarchiv/age fotostock; 24 right: stefbennett/Getty Images; 25 left: JJ Harrison/Wikimedia; 25 right: Xinhua/Shutterstock; 26 main: Afanasievich/Fotosearch LBRF/age fotostock; 26 top inset: Picture by Tambako the Jaguar/Getty Images; 27 top left: Stefan Huwiler/Getty Images; 29 bottom: VR19/Getty Images; 30–31 bottom: Louis Brems/Quad City Times/AP Images; 33: brittak/Getty Images; 35 right: Sven-Erik Arndt/imageBROKER/Shutterstock; 36 center left: Charles Christian Nahl/Wikimedia; 36 center right: JOSE ANTONIO PEÑAS/Science Source; 36 right: Claus Lunau/Science Source; 37 left: North Wind Picture Archives/Alamy Images; 37 center: Topical Press Agency/Getty Images; 37 right foreground: Sundry Photography/Getty Images; 38: Waltraud Grubitzsch/picture-alliance/dpa/AP Images; 39: Jessica Reilly/Telegraph Herald/AP Images; 40 sign: Mark Newman/Getty Images; 40–41 background: billnoll/Getty Images; 42–43 all: Courtesy of the Fred Family; 44: Louis Brems/Quad City Times/AP Images.

All other photos © Shutterstock.